The School Rules

RULES IN THE LIBRARY

By Paul Bloom

Gareth Stevens
PUBLISHING

Please visit our website, www.garethstevens.com. For a free color catalog of all our high-quality books, call toll free 1-800-542-2595 or fax 1-877-542-2596.

Library of Congress Cataloging-in-Publication Data

Bloom, Paul.
Rules in the library / by Paul Bloom.
p. cm. — (The school rules)
Includes index.
ISBN 978-1-4824-2649-6 (pbk.)
ISBN 978-1-4824-2650-2 (6 pack)
ISBN 978-1-4824-2651-9 (library binding)
1. Library etiquette — Juvenile literature. 2. Schools — Juvenile literature. 3. Etiquette for children and teenagers — Juvenile literature. I. Bloom, Paul, 1963-. II. Title.
Z716.43 B56 2016
027—d23

First Edition

Published in 2016 by
Gareth Stevens Publishing
111 East 14th Street, Suite 349
New York, NY 10003

Editor: Ryan Nagelhout
Designer: Laura Bowen

Photo credits: Cover, p. 1 Christopher Futcher/E+/Getty Images; pp. 5, 24 (library) Protasov AN/Shutterstock.com; pp. 7, 9, 11, 21 wavebreakmedia/Shutterstock.com; p. 13 © iStockphoto.com/kali9; pp. 15, 23, 24 (librarian) Tyler Olson/Shutterstock.com; pp. 17, 24 (computer) Hung Chung Chih/Shutterstock.com; p. 19 Andersen Ross/Blend Images/Getty Images.

Printed in the United States of America

CPSIA compliance information: Batch #CS15GS: For further information contact Gareth Stevens, New York, New York at 1-800-542-2595.

Contents

My school has
a library.

I go there
with my class.

We follow the rules.

You have to be quiet.
People are trying
to read!

Do not run around.

A person there
helps you find books.
This is a librarian.

You can also use a computer to find books.

Find a nice chair
to read in.

Ask to take
your books home!

Be sure to bring
them back!
This is called lending.